Published by Barbour Publishing, Inc., P.O. Box 719, Uhrichsville, Ohio 44683
http://www.barbourbooks.com

Member of the
Evangelical Christian
Publishers Association

Printed in China.

May you sense His peace in this difficult time

ELLYN SANNA

BARBOUR
PUBLISHING, INC.

Peace I leave with you;
my peace I give you.
I do not give to you as the world gives.
Do not let your hearts be troubled
and do not be afraid.

JOHN 14:27 NIV

One

You Are Not Alone

Small sadnesses, great tragedies,
link us all in love.

PAM BROWN

No one can develop freely in this world
and find a full life without feeling
understood by at least one person.

PAUL TORNIER

I know I've never experienced exactly what you're feeling now. But please know that others share your pain. Come to me whenever you want. I promise to do my best to understand.

Sometimes we try so hard to be strong. We don't want others to see how weak we really are. We don't want to be a burden.

But those of us who love you want to do anything we can to help. Please give us a chance to show how much we love you.

Trouble is part of your life,
and if you don't share it,
you don't give the person who loves you
a chance to love you enough.

DINAH SHORE

Think of one thing.
You are not alone.
A million million lives have known
this pain—and found at last a way
to new tranquility.

PAM BROWN

When you're hurting, sometimes it seems as though you've been abandoned, stranded in a world of pain. But you are not alone. Others have felt the sorrow you feel now—and they have survived. In the midst of this difficult time, they have found a new sense of God's peace.

I'm praying that you, too, will feel that peace.

When others. . .are sad,
share their sorrow.

ROMANS 12:15 NLT

When you find yourself in the valley of shadow. . .
feel His gentle touch in those loving hugs,
those silent pats on the back when words fail,
those acts of love and caring,
and especially the prayers of support.
In all these we know His presence.

ELDYN SIMONS

For as the sufferings of Christ abound in us,
so our consolation also abounds through Christ.

2 CORINTHIANS 1:5 NKJV

Where there is sorrow, where there is pain, where
there is fear—there loving-kindness grows and flowers.

PAM BROWN

For we are joined together in his body
by his strong sinews.

COLOSSIANS 2:19 NLT

I know we're two separate people. I can never completely share your feelings. But in another sense, we are united; we are one in Christ. And because we are united, a part of Christ's body can't be hurt without the entire body hurting, too.

I hurt for you. I share your pain. Let me know what I can do to help.

That we may be able to comfort
those who are in any trouble,
with the comfort with which
we ourselves are comforted by God.

2 CORINTHIANS 1:4 NKJV

Two

God Is with You Even Now

"My Presence will go with you,
and I will give you rest."

EXODUS 33:14 NIV

Sometimes it seems as though God has left us all alone. Life seems just too hard, too terrible; it's more than we can bear, and God's presence doesn't seem to be anywhere.

But God will never leave you all alone, even though you may feel that way. He is with you in the midst of this hard time. His love for you will never go away.

God walks with us. . . . He scoops us up in His arms
or simply sits with us in silent strength
until we cannot avoid the awesome recognition
that yes, even now, He is here.

GLORIA GAITHER

*God will never let you be shaken or moved
from your place near His heart.*

JONI EARECKSON TADA

Have confidence in God's mercy, for when you think
He is a long way from you, He is often quite near.

THOMAS À KEMPIS

*I*t is of great importance that you endeavour, at all times, to keep your hearts in peace; that you may keep pure that temple of God. The way to keep it in peace is to enter into it by means of inward silence. When you see yourself more sharply assaulted, retreat into that region of peace; and you will find a fortress that will enable you to triumph over all your enemies, visible and invisible, and over all their snares and temptations. Within your own soul resides divine aid and sovereign succour. Retreat within it, and all will be quiet, secure, peaceable, and calm. Thus, by means of mental silence, which can only be attained with divine help, you may look for tranquility in tumult; for solitude in company; for light in darkness; for forgetfulness in pressures; for vigour in despondency; for courage in fear; for resistance in temptation; and for quiet in tribulation.

WILLIAM BACKHOUSE AND JAMES JANSEN

The LORD is close to the brokenhearted
and saves those who are crushed in spirit.

PSALM 34:18 NIV

*Jesus cannot forget us; we have been
graven on the palms of His hands.*

LOIS PICILLO

God is our refuge and strength,
an ever-present help in trouble.
Therefore we will not fear. . . .
The LORD Almighty is with us.

PSALM 46:1–2, 7 NIV

Can anything ever separate us from Christ's love? Does it mean he no longer loves us if we have trouble or calamity, or are persecuted, or are hungry or cold or in danger or threatened with death? . . . No, despite all these things, overwhelming victory is ours through Christ, who loved us.

And I am convinced that nothing can ever separate us from his love. Death can't, and life can't. The angels can't, and the demons can't. Our fears for today, our worries about tomorrow, and even the powers of hell can't keep God's love away. . . . Nothing in all creation will ever be able to separate us from the love of God that is revealed in Christ Jesus our Lord.

ROMANS 8:35, 37–39 NLT

Three

God Feels Your Pain

A teardrop on earth summons the King of heaven.

CHARLES R. SWINDOLL

Jesus is holding His arms out to you right now, longing to give you peace. "I feel your tears, My child," He's saying. "You are not alone. My own heart is crying with you. That's why I came to earth—so I could share your pain."

When no one else can really understand, know that God understands. I'm praying that you will sense His comforting arms around you. You are so precious to Him.

Regardless of the need, God comforts.
He is the God of all comfort!
That's His specialty.

CHARLES R. SWINDOLL

Not a sigh is breathed, not a pain felt,
not a grief pierces the soul
but the throb vibrates to the Father's heart.

ELLEN G. WHITE

"How could God let something like this happen?" we ask ourselves. "Why didn't He protect us from this trouble?"

But in this life we will never understand why so much pain fills our world. All we can do is trust that God is with us in our suffering. He does not watch us from heaven, far away from our troubles. No, He is here with us; His presence surrounds us even in the darkest times.

And when our hearts are breaking, His heart breaks, too.

God's comfort restores and heals the hurting soul.
It lifts the crushed and broken spirit.
It brings again a sense of worth and purpose
when all seems empty and dark.
Comfort is the touch of God when we thought
we were all alone in our night.
It is the promise that dawn is on its way.

ELDYN SIMONS

Somehow, someday, God will bring His peace to you. There is no night so dark, no trouble so deep, that He will not shine the light of His presence even there.

Wait for God. Trust Him to bring His comfort to your heart.

Four

Rely On God's Strength To Get You Through

God's peace. . .is far more wonderful than the human mind can understand. His peace will keep your thoughts and your hearts quiet and at rest.

PHILIPPIANS 4:7 TLB

We must take our troubles to the Lord,
but we must do more than that;
we must leave them there.

HANNAH WHITALL SMITH

Snuggle in God's arms.
When you are hurting, when you feel lonely...
let Him cradle you, comfort you, reassure you
of His all-sufficient power and love.

KAY ARTHUR

Let him have all your worries and cares,
for he is always thinking about you
and watching everything that concerns you.

1 PETER 5:7 TLB

I call on you, O God,
for you will answer me. . . .
Keep me as the apple of your eye;
hide me under the shadow of your wings.

PSALM 17:6, 8 NIV

But how shall we rest in God? By giving ourselves
wholly to Him. If you give yourself by halves, you
cannot find full rest—there will ever be a lurking
disquiet in that half which is withheld. . . . All peace
and happiness in this world depend upon unreserved
self-oblation to God. If this be hearty and entire,
the result will be an unfailing, ever-increasing
happiness, which nothing can disturb. There is no
real happiness in this life save that which is
the result of a peaceful heart.

JEAN N. GROU

To thee, O God, we turn for peace; but grant us, too,
the blessed assurance that nothing shall deprive us
of that peace, neither ourselves, nor our foolish,
earthly desires, nor my wild longings,
nor the anxious cravings of my heart.

SOREN KIERKEGAARD

*See in the meantime that your faith
bringeth forth obedience,
and God in due time will cause it
to bring forth peace.*

JOHN OWEN

Peace does not mean
the end of all our striving,
Joy does not mean
the drying of our tears.
Peace is the power that
comes to souls arriving
Up to the light where God
Himself appears.

G. A. STUDDERT KENNEDY

Nothing can separate you from God's love,
absolutely nothing. . . . God is enough for time,
God is enough for eternity.
God is enough!

HANNAH WHITALL SMITH

*God can do wonders with a broken heart
if you give Him all the pieces.*

VICTOR ALFSEN

Heavenly Father, God of all mercies and comfort,
in the midst of this awfulness that has come to me,
I am certain that You are here and that You really care
about me. Hold me close, Lord. Let me feel Your
great love. Help me to know without question that
even this trial has come through the permissive grace
of Your love for me. Help me to know that You care
when I feel so alone and so blinded by the darkness. . . .
As I ran to my parents, I now run to You, Lord.
I don't understand, but I trust You to make it better.
May I feel Your touch. Hold me steady. Reassure me.
Give me Your comfort. Let me experience the
healing touch of Your love. Amen.

ELDYN SIMONS, THE DAWN OF HOPE

Ask God for peace
and see what a transformation
will take place in your life.

BILLY GRAHAM

This world can and may take everything you have. But no one can take away your faith.

MAX LUCADO

When all else is gone,
God is left, and nothing changes Him.

HANNAH WHITALL SMITH

Cast your burden on the LORD,
and he will sustain you.

PSALM 55:22 NRSV

Come to Me, all you who labor and are heavy laden,
and I will give you rest.

MATTHEW 11:28 NKJV

When it seems you can take no more, the One who loves you will come to your rescue. Rely on Him. When the storms overwhelm you, God is there, and He is faithful. He will provide you with the strength you need to carry your burdens; He will hide you in His own heart, giving you shelter against even the fiercest storm.

You are my hiding place;
you will protect me from trouble
and surround me with songs of deliverance.

PSALM 32:7 NIV

Five

Joy Comes in the Morning

Weeping may endure for a night,
but joy cometh in the morning.

PSALM 30:5 KJV

Those who plant in tears
will harvest with shouts of joy.
They weep as they go to plant their seed,
but they sing as they return with the harvest.

PSALM 126:5-6 NLT

We can be assured of this:
God, who knows all and sees all,
will set all things straight in the end.
Even better, He will dry every tear.

RICHARD J. FOSTER

Out of every crisis comes the chance to be reborn. . .to
choose the kind of change that will help us to grow. . . .

NENO O'NEILL

In the depth of winter, I finally learned that
within me there lay an invincible spring.

ALBERT CAMUS

*Out of suffering have emerged the
strongest souls; the most massive characters
are seamed with scars.*

E. H. CHAPIN

How can we shout for joy? . . . And yet somehow,
someway, God will not only ease our pain
but replace it with a joy so bright and exuberant
that we'll want to shout. . . . Behind the dark clouds,
God's hope shines like the sun.

ELDYN SIMONS

Even as the stone of the fruit must break,
that its heart may stand in the sun,
so must you know pain.

KAHLIL GIBRAN

Remember when Jesus spoke of the grain of wheat that had to fall into the ground and die before it could grow? I believe that's what's happening in your life today: Your outer shell is being cracked open, so that new green life can grow up into the light. I know this time is hard. But one day, who knows how rich a harvest you will reap?

The world calls you back to life.
Listen.
The shrill of bird song.
A river breaking from the ice.
Rain after drought.
Sunshine after cloud.

PAM BROWN

*If it were not for hopes,
the heart would break.*

THOMAS FULLER

$\mathcal{P}$ierre Renoir, the famous artist, suffered from terrible arthritis as he grew older. His hands were stiff and clumsy, and the smallest movement caused him pain. And yet he never stopped painting. When he was asked how he could persevere in the face of such hardship, he responded, "The pain passes, but the beauty remains."

One day, your pain will also pass. But nothing can ever rob you of the beauty God has created in your life.

When they walk through the
Valley of Weeping,
it will become a place of refreshing springs,
where pools of blessing collect after the rains!

PSALM 84:6 NLT

The earth is empty. The trees, once thick with blossom,
stand dead against a bitter sky. The streams are frozen.
But see—along the branches new buds appear and
greenness pushes through the ground unnoticed.
Spring may be slow—but will at last return.

PAM BROWN

*The rainbow of God's promises is always
above the trials and storms of life.*

CHARLES SHEPSON

I'm so sorry you have to face this hard time right now. But I'm praying that out of the dark clouds that fill your life you'll see the lovely arch of a rainbow. May you feel the sense of hope that every rainbow brings.

And may that hope bring you peace.

*There is a way out of every dark mist,
over a rainbow trail.*

NAVAJO SONG